MP Middleton Press

EVOLVING THE ULTIMATE RAIL ENCYCLOPEDIA

Easebourne Lane, Midhurst, West Sussex.
GU29 9AZ   Tel:01730 813169
www.middletonpress.co.uk   email:info@middletonpress.co.uk
A-978 0 906520   B- 978 1 873793   C- 978 1 901706   D-978 1 904474
E - 978 1 906008   F - 978 1 908174

All titles listed below were in print at time of publication - please check current availability by looking at our website - *www.middletonpress.co.uk* or by requesting a Brochure which includes our *LATEST* RAILWAY TITLES also our TRAMWAY, TROLLEYBUS, MILITARY and WATERWAYS series

WESTERN **BRITISH RAILWAYS** REGION

THROUGH TRAIN SERVICE
Swansea, Llanelly,
Carmarthen, Aberystwyth,
Barmouth and Penychain (BUTLIN'S HOLIDAY CAMP)

WITH CONNECTIONS FROM AND TO OTHER SOUTH WALES STATIONS

SATURDAYS ONLY

SUMMER, 1959

JUNE 20th TO AUGUST 29th (incl.)				JUNE 27th TO SEPTEMBER 5th (incl.)			
			a.m.				a.m.
NEWPORT	..	dep.	7 32	PWLLHELI	.. ..	dep.	10 A 0
CARDIFF (General)	..	,,	8 0	PENYCHAIN	.. ..	,,	10 18
BRIDGEND	..	,,	8 32	AFON WEN	.. ..	,,	10 23
PORT TALBOT (General)	,,		9 0	CRICCIETH	.. ..	,,	10 33
BRITON FERRY	..	,,	9 8	PORTMADOC	.. ..	,,	10 43
NEATH (General)	..	,,	9 14	HARLECH	.. ..	,,	11 0
SWANSEA (High Street)	arr.		9 38	BARMOUTH	.. .. { arr.		11 23
					{ dep.		11 28
			a.m.				p.m.
SWANSEA (High Street)	dep.		10 10	TOWYN	..	,,	12 2
COCKETT	..	,,	10 20	ABERDOVEY	..	,,	12 12
GOWERTON (North)	..	,,	10 25	ABERYSTWYTH	.. { arr.		1 20
LOUGHOR	..	,,	10 30		{ dep.		1 45
LLANELLY	..	,,	10 40	LAMPETER	.. ..	,,	2 49
PEMBREY & BURRY PORT	,,		10 49	PENCADER	.. ..		3 16
KIDWELLY	..	,,	10 58	CARMARTHEN	..	arr.	3 55
FERRYSIDE	..	,,	11 6				
CARMARTHEN	.. { arr.		11 20				p.m.
	{ dep.		11 35	CARMARTHEN	..	dep.	4 10
			p.m.	FERRYSIDE	..	arr.	4 22
PENCADER	..		12 14	KIDWELLY	..	,,	4 30
LAMPETER	..		12 39	PEMBREY & BURRY PORT	,,		4 39
ABERYSTWYTH	.. { arr.		1 35	LLANELLY	..	,,	4 50
	{ dep.		1 40	LOUGHOR	..	,,	4 57
ABERDOVEY	..		2 48	GOWERTON (North)	..	,,	5 2
TOWYN	..		2 58	COCKETT	..	,,	5 10
BARMOUTH	.. { arr.		3 40	SWANSEA (High Street)	..	,,	5 18
	{ dep.		3 46	NEATH (General)	..	,,	5 45
HARLECH	..	arr.	4 8	BRITON FERRY	..	,,	6 B 37
PORTMADOC	..	,,	4 28	PORT TALBOT (General)	,,		6 0
CRICCIETH	..	,,	4 44	BRIDGEND	..	,,	6 20
AFON WEN	..	,,	4 51	CARDIFF (General)	..	,,	6 52
PENYCHAIN	..	,,	4 56	NEWPORT	..	,,	7 17
PWLLHELI	..	,,	5 5				

Through Train Swansea (High St.) to Pwllheli

Through Train Penychain to Carmarthen

A—Change at Afon Wen. **B**—Change at Swansea (High Street).

Paddington Station, W.2.
April, 1959.

J. R. HAMMOND,
General Manager.

Printed in Great Britain by C. E. Watkins Ltd., Green Dragon Lane, Swansea. T.E. 1476

LLANDYFRIOG

120.   *Sgt Murphy* has reached the end of the line on 29th May 2001 and is about to run round its train. The station came into use on 24th March 1990. The line was extended a further 600yds on 1st April 2006 to the river at Pont Teifi. Riverside was the name given to the station. (P.G.Barnes)

119.   The new platform was opened on the site of the southern GWR one on 18th July 2009, consent having long been refused owing to the curvature. (TVR)

118.   The platform edge in the foreground has been seen previously, on the right of picture 102. *Sgt Murphy* is propelling empty stock towards the shed on 29th May 2001. The signal box was a recent arrival from Caerphilly Works preservation site, but was originally at Rhiwderin on the Brecon & Merthyr line. The frame went to the Gwili Railway. It was later moved to the side of the yard. (P.G.Barnes)

117.   A panorama from 12th June 1994 has 0-4-0ST *Woto* on the left. It was a visitor from Alan Keefe's works at Ross-on-Wye. Hunslet 0-4-0ST *Alan George,* whose centenary was being celebrated, is on the right. (T.Heavyside)

5. Teifi Valley Railway

HENLLAN

116.   More than nine miles of trackbed were purchased in 1981 on which to lay a nominal 2ft gauge railway. Operation began on 24th August 1985, the new platform being on the opposite side of the road bridge from the old ones. Seen on 11th June 1994 is Kerr Stuart 0-6-2T *Sgt Murphy* of 1918. The first terminus was at Pontprenshitw. (T.Heavyside)

XXXV.   Route diagram in 2010. Two platforms are shown at Henllan, the one on the right having been added in 2009. Forest Halt opened in December 1987.

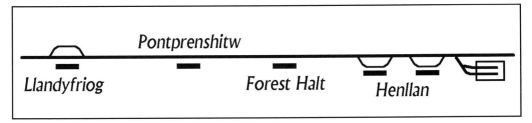

Pontprenshitw

Llandyfriog   Forest Halt   Henllan

DANYCOED

115.   Extension to Danycoed took place on 31st March 2001. The 12.30pm from Bronwydd Arms was hauled by 0-6-0ST no. 68011 on 29th May 2001. Named *Errol Lonsdale*, this locomotive had spent much of its life working on the Longmoor Military Railway. (P.G.Barnes)

LLWYFAN CERRIG

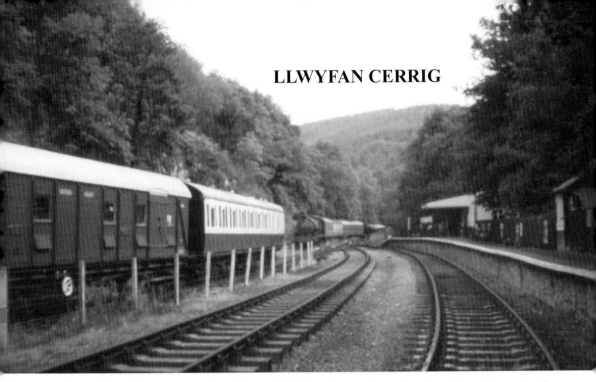

113.　　This station was opened on 17th April 1987 and was built on the site of Conwil stone loading dock. Seen on 5th September 1995 is *Sir John* again. (M.Dart)

114.　　Working the 13.00 from Danycoed on 13th June 2009 is 0-6-0ST *Haulwen*, a 1945 product of the Vulcan Foundry. The station building had previously served at Felin Fach. The locomotive shed is in the background. (P.G.Barnes)

112.   Seen in the distance in September 1995 is the reconstructed signal box, which had earlier served at Llandybie. The locomotive is *Sir John*, an Avonside 0-6-0ST of 1914. (M.Dart)

4. Gwili Railway

BRONWYDD ARMS

111. The trackbed was acquired in October 1977 and some operations began at Easter 1978. This southward view from 25th July 1993 includes a building which had formerly served as the signal box at Llandovery and as the station building at Ammanford Town. (M.J.Stretton)

XXXIV. Track diagram in 2010.

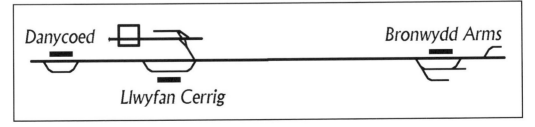

110.   Seen on 12th September 1970 is the "Milk Branches Rail Tour" described in caption 31. The day trip cost 50 shillings. Fertilisers, coal and oil were the main commodities handled here. (M.Dart)

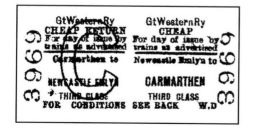

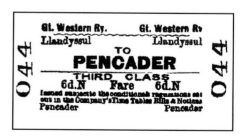

108.   The symmetrical exterior was recorded on the same day. The more important stations of the era were adorned with much decorative ironwork. The plan was similar to that at Ross-on-Wye. (H.C.Casserley)

109.   The yard was still busy on 3rd March 1962, but the cattle dock was to be seldom used again. Goods traffic continued until 22nd September 1973. (P.J.Garland/R.S.Carpenter coll.)

106.　The siding on the right of the previous view continues to the turntable and the engine shed. They were all removed in 1960, the shed having closed in September 1952. (R.S.Carpenter)

107.　Shunting on 9th July 1958 is 0-6-0PT no. 9632, fuel tankers always being in evidence. This is the panorama from the signal box steps. (R.M.Casserley)

105.   Moving further away from the station, we see much of the goods yard, in September 1952. The signal box is almost obscured by foliage, strictly contrary to the Rule Book. It had 17 levers and functioned until 25th November 1956. (R.S.Carpenter)

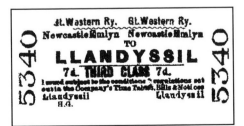

104.   A panorama from August 1948 includes a cattle wagon in the dock on the left. There were cattle pens to the left of it. (Lens of Sutton coll.)

Newcastle Emlyn	1903	1913	1923	1933
Passenger tickets issued	18669	24750	25084	8236
Season tickets issued	*	*	60	50
Parcels forwarded	9139	19913	20780	22098
General goods forwarded (tons)	684	1373	3740	371
Coal and coke received (tons)	3939	2878	2000	1664
Other minerals received (tons)	1206	2031	5688	1743
General goods received (tons)	4171	5083	6269	6106
Trucks of livestock handled	867	917	743	347

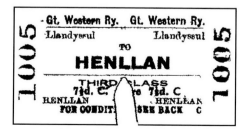

NEWCASTLE EMLYN

XXXIII.   The 1911 survey shows the proximity of the terminus to the river and the county boundary, which is in the centre of it. The town had a population of 855 in 1901, which fell to 655 in 1961.

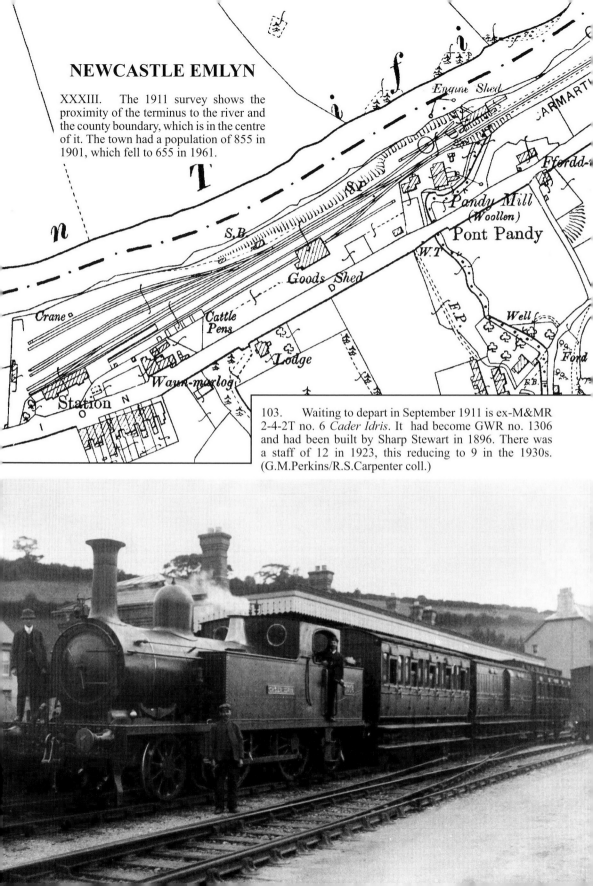

103.   Waiting to depart in September 1911 is ex-M&MR 2-4-2T no. 6 *Cader Idris*. It had become GWR no. 1306 and had been built by Sharp Stewart in 1896. There was a staff of 12 in 1923, this reducing to 9 in the 1930s. (G.M.Perkins/R.S.Carpenter coll.)

Henllan	1903	1913	1923	1933
Passenger tickets issued	15906	17716	15688	10779
Season tickets issued	*	*	88	35
Parcels forwarded	6114	11644	15159	9245
General goods forwarded (tons)	1366	627	790	343
Coal and coke received (tons)	2433	2806	3115	2407
Other minerals received (tons)	427	629	1365	1352
General goods received (tons)	2195	2799	3097	3061
Trucks of livestock handled	207	189	228	213

101.   More activity is seen on the same day, but from the opposite direction. The crane was rated at 6 tons lifting capacity and the goods yard closed on 6th September 1965. (R.M.Casserley)

102.   The 23-lever signal box had been replaced by two ground frames on 25th November 1956. The 11.25am freight from Newcastle Emlyn was hauled by 0-6-0PT no. 9606 on 18th August 1962. See pictures 115 onwards for the story of the new railway which runs west from this site. (J.Langford)

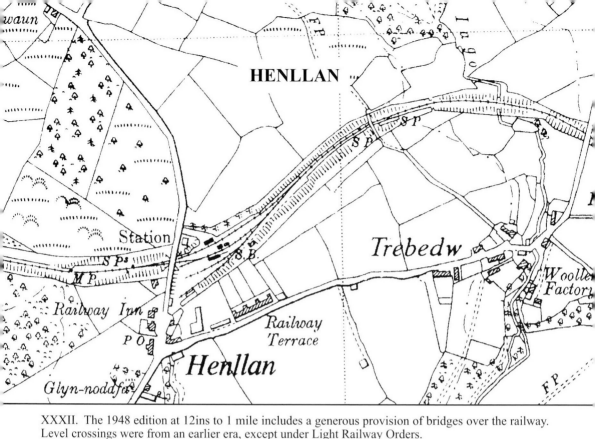

XXXII. The 1948 edition at 12ins to 1 mile includes a generous provision of bridges over the railway. Level crossings were from an earlier era, except under Light Railway Orders.

100.   Shunting on 9th July 1958 is 0-6-0PT no. 9632. By that time, the barrow crossing at the east end had rotted, but the buildings were all complete. There had been seven employees here in the 1930s. (R.M.Casserley)

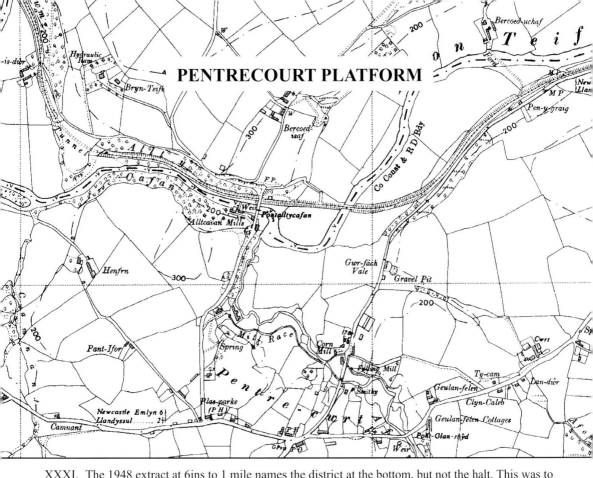

PENTRECOURT PLATFORM

XXXI. The 1948 extract at 6ins to 1 mile names the district at the bottom, but not the halt. This was to the right of the word "Weir" and its hut is marked. Alltycafan Tunnel, which was 167yds long, is on the left. Above it is a hydraulic ram, a then common water powered water pump.

99.   Crowds turned out for the opening day on 1st February 1912, since when a GWR Pagoda shelter graced the scene. (Lens of Sutton coll.)

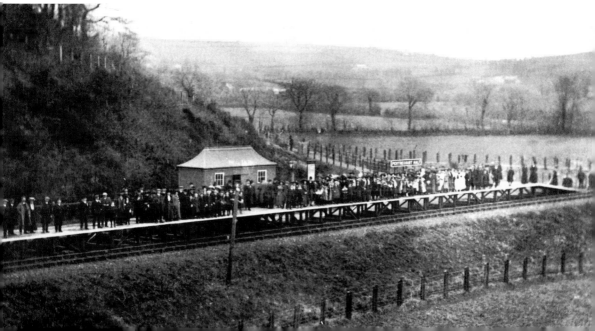

98.   A westward panorama on 18th August 1962 includes the 1894 signal box, which had 27 levers and was in use until 25th November 1956. It was replaced by two ground frames. Goods traffic ceased on 6th September 1965. (J.Langford)

Llandyssul	1903	1913	1923	1933
Passenger tickets issued	21241	46406	24241	4946
Season tickets issued	*	*	33	11
Parcels forwarded	12632	21478	25805	25395
General goods forwarded (tons)	987	1487	1333	809
Coal and coke received (tons)	3555	3892	2545	2267
Other minerals received (tons)	1274	1947	2623	2345
General goods received (tons)	6210	6774	7056	7694
Trucks of livestock handled	335	278	692	325

96.   The unsupported canopy was an excellent GWR design. Its goods shed is in the background of this 1957 picture, while the new agricultural store is on staddle stones on the left. There had been a turntable in the right background until 1896. (D.K.Jones coll.)

97.   The former entrance was recorded on 9th July 1958. The white corner to the platform side of the building was a legacy to the blackout of World War II. White platform edges also arrived at that time. (H.C.Casserley)

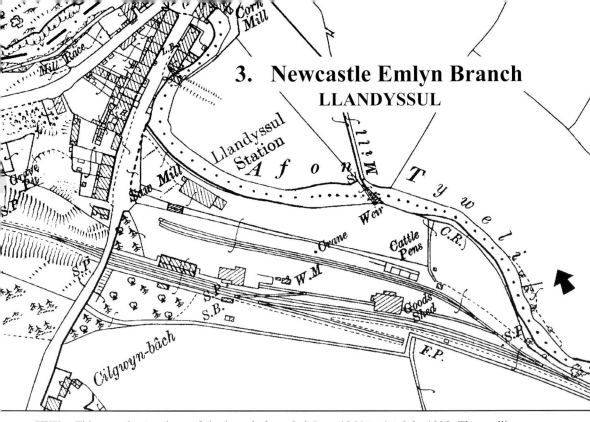

3. Newcastle Emlyn Branch
LLANDYSSUL

XXX.   This was the terminus of the branch from 3rd June 1864 to 1st July 1895. The spelling was Llandyssil until 17th December 1918 and Llandyssul until April 1957 after which time one "s" was deemed sufficient. We use the last form quoted to passengers, such services ending on 15th September 1952.

95.   This postcard recorded market day, probably in about 1912. The Anglo American Oil Company was supplying the developing motor trade and petrol was unloaded into cans, to be purchased over the counter in shops. Pumps were in their infancy. Eleven men were employed in the 1930s.
(Lens of Sutton coll.)

94.   The same locomotive was recorded on 15th July 1961, outside the small shed, which was in use until April 1962. It had served at Wrexham Central until 1925. (A.M.Davies)

92.   The GWR established bus routes from here to Lampeter and to Aberystwyth in 1906, adding one to New Quay in 1907. Such services outlasted the branch and Western Welsh Leylands adorn the yard on 18th July 1958. (F.Hornby)

93.   The shed in the background was assembled from concrete sections in 1956 and housed bagged fertilisers and feedstuffs. No. 7402 is taking water in about 1960; note the "fire devil" to prevent the pipe freezing. (D.K.Jones coll.)

90.   It is about 1957 and all was still intact, although the last passenger had left six years earlier. The crane is on the right and was rated at 30cwt. It was used to load much timber, particularly pit props. (R.G.Nelson/T.Walsh)

91.   Much of the fencing was removed after 1951 to facilitate parcel handling. There had earlier been a regular school train as far as Felin Fach. (W.A.Camwell/SLS coll.)

88.   Staff pose for a postcard photographer, as a train is about to leave in around 1905. A staff of
6 or 7 was normal in the 1930s. A weighing machine was added in 1912.
(Lens of Sutton coll.)

89.   This splendid panorama is from around 1912 and includes an autotrain having just run near the
connection to the engine shed. The small signal box contained six levers and functioned until 6th May
1965, when traffic ceased. Camping coaches were sited to the left of the water tower in 1932-39 and
1952-62. See the lower picture on the back cover. (Lens of Sutton coll.)

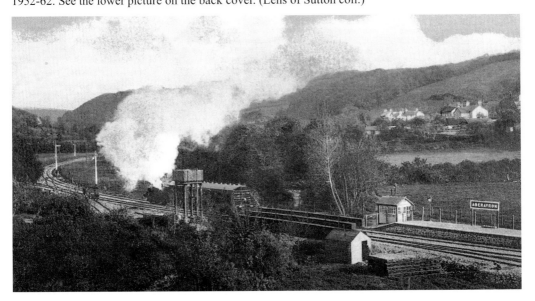

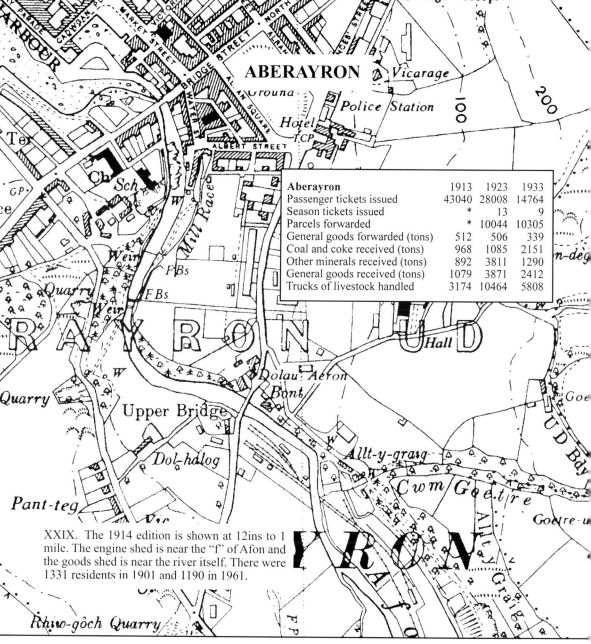

ABERAYRON

Aberayron	1913	1923	1933
Passenger tickets issued	43040	28008	14764
Season tickets issued	*	13	9
Parcels forwarded	*	10044	10305
General goods forwarded (tons)	512	506	339
Coal and coke received (tons)	968	1085	2151
Other minerals received (tons)	892	3811	1290
General goods received (tons)	1079	3871	2412
Trucks of livestock handled	3174	10464	5808

XXIX. The 1914 edition is shown at 12ins to 1 mile. The engine shed is near the "f" of Afon and the goods shed is near the river itself. There were 1331 residents in 1901 and 1190 in 1961.

87.   We look south at the station nearing completion in the Winter of 1910-11 and see the new bridge *over* the river on the left. The map suggests the reverse to be the case. (Lens of Sutton coll.)

CROSSWAYS HALT

85.   The halt opened on 8th April 1929 and we look inland at the remains on 7th July 1958. (H.C.Casserley)

LLANERCH AYRON HALT

86.   The halt came into use a little after the branch, on 2nd October 1911. It is seen from the west in July 1958, in use as a rail store. (H.C.Casserley)

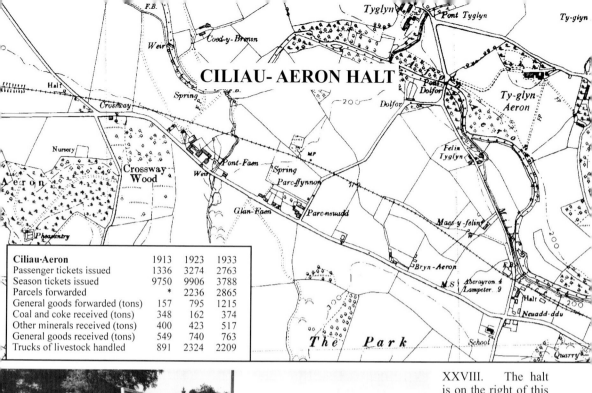

CILIAU-AERON HALT

Ciliau-Aeron	1913	1923	1933
Passenger tickets issued	1336	3274	2763
Season tickets issued	9750	9906	3788
Parcels forwarded	*	2236	2865
General goods forwarded (tons)	157	795	1215
Coal and coke received (tons)	348	162	374
Other minerals received (tons)	400	423	517
General goods received (tons)	549	740	763
Trucks of livestock handled	891	2324	2209

XXVIII. The halt is on the right of this 1948 map at 6ins to 1 mile. On the left of it, and also on map XXVI, is Crossways Halt, which is seen in picture 85. "Aeron" was added in about 1912 and "Halt" was not used in 1936-39.

83. We look west on 30th August 1951. There had been a staff of one in most years. A housing estate now occupies the site. (W.A.Camwell/ SLS coll.)

84. An eastward view from 7th July 1958 shows that little had changed. Freight continued until 2nd December 1963, there being a ground frame at both ends of the loop. (H.C.Casserley)

81.   Green Grove Siding was on the south side of the branch and opened on 10th May 1951 to serve the Milk Marketing Board's depot. The two photographs are from 7th July 1958 and they include 0-6-0PT no. 7444. (H.C.Casserley)

82.   There was a ground frame at each end of the loop and traffic continued until 1st October 1973, but the line westwards closed to freight on 5th April 1965. (H.C.Casserley)

79.   It is 11th June 1964 and the nine-lever signal box had just been reduced to a ground frame and the loop on the left taken out of use. The loop in the distance is still busy and lasted until April 1965. (P.J.Garland/R.S.Carpenter coll.)

80.   Seen on the same day is the east end of the former loop. The station building was acquired by the Gwili Railway Preservation Society and was moved to Llwyfan Cerrig around 1989. (P.J.Garland/R.S.Carpenter coll.)

77.　　The parcels shed is included in this westward view of the 9.47am goods train from Lampeter, hauled by 0-6-0PT no. 7444 on 7th July 1958. (H.C.Casserley)

78.　　A different view of the same train includes the cattle dock and the 30cwt crane. There was a loop at the platforms and also one here. (H.C.Casserley)

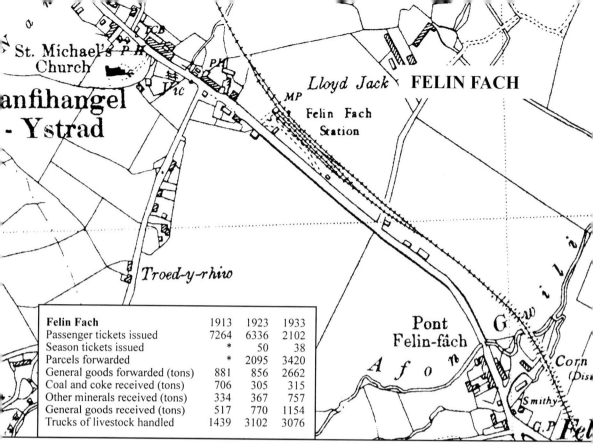

Felin Fach	1913	1923	1933
Passenger tickets issued	7264	6336	2102
Season tickets issued	*	50	38
Parcels forwarded	*	2095	3420
General goods forwarded (tons)	881	856	2662
Coal and coke received (tons)	706	305	315
Other minerals received (tons)	334	367	757
General goods received (tons)	517	770	1154
Trucks of livestock handled	1439	3102	3076

XXVII. The 1948 edition at 12ins to 1 mile explains why the station was called Ystrad initially. It was changed on 1st January 1913, as Ystrad was used elsewhere on the GWR.

76.   Taken within the first two years, this fine photograph features a class 517 0-4-2T, with an autocoach. There were two employees here in the 1930s. (GWR)

XXVI. The 1952 edition at 1ins to 1 mile shows the first six stops on the branch, although just closed.

BLAENPLWYF HALT

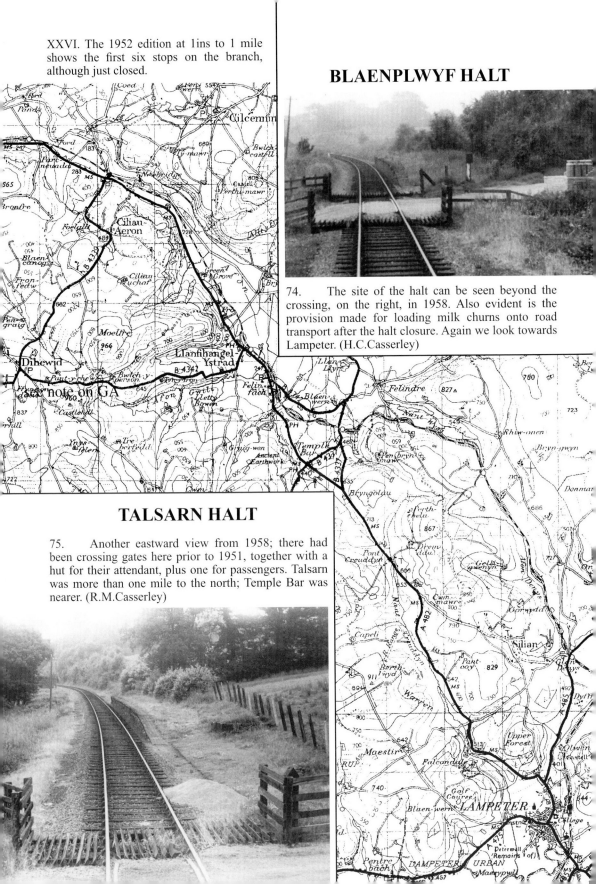

74.   The site of the halt can be seen beyond the crossing, on the right, in 1958. Also evident is the provision made for loading milk churns onto road transport after the halt closure. Again we look towards Lampeter. (H.C.Casserley)

TALSARN HALT

75.   Another eastward view from 1958; there had been crossing gates here prior to 1951, together with a hut for their attendant, plus one for passengers. Talsarn was more than one mile to the north; Temple Bar was nearer. (R.M.Casserley)

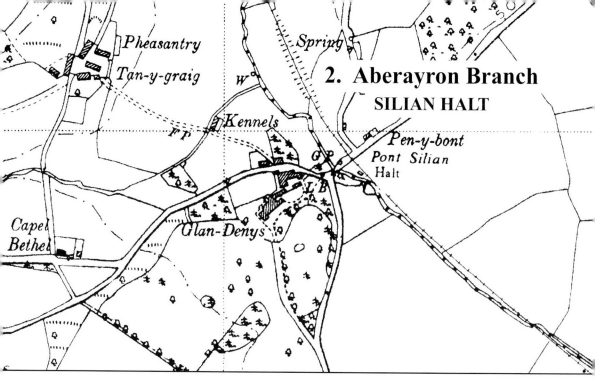

XXV.   The location is shown on the 1948 edition at 12ins to 1 mile. Silian was over ½ mile to the west. "Halt" was used from 1938.

73.   Aberayron Junction is described in caption 37 and is on the right of map XXVI. The branch closed to passengers on 12th February 1951 and the halt is seen on 7th July 1958, looking towards Lampeter. There had been a goods siding here until 7th March 1943. (H.C.Casserley)

71.   A southward panorama from May 1961 has the up goods loop in the centre. The platforms on the left were extended in 1931 to form an island, giving three through platforms and two bays. A private siding for milk traffic was provided on the left in 1929 and was used into the 1970s. (D.K.Jones coll.)

72.   No. 7405 takes water in the down bay on 23rd March 1962, while we marvel at the scale of the 1931 bridge, which also extended across the river. The approach ramp to the station (left) came at the same time. There is now no railway beyond the bridge, but two platforms remain usable. (M.A.N.Johnston)

Other pictures of the area can be found in *Llandeilo to Swansea* (nos 117 to 120), *Carmarthen to Fishguard* (nos 1 to 10) and *Swansea to Carmarthen* (nos 69-82).

↙ 68. A view north from the new footbridge includes the old road bridge and and also the prison. The level crossing is just beyond the train and the roof of the 1902 signal box can be seen. Station Box was at the south end of the main platform until closure on 6th May 1972. (Lens of Sutton coll.)

69. A 1947 panorama shows the north end layout from 1931. The train in the bay platform is probably bound for Llandeilo. (W.A.Camwell/SLS coll.)

70. The 1907 engine shed is seen from the south in June 1958, with 0-6-0 no. 2273 on the left. The workshop is behind it and a 65ft turntable is out of view, on the right. The shed had the code 87G and closed in April 1964. (N.K.Harrop/Bentley coll.)

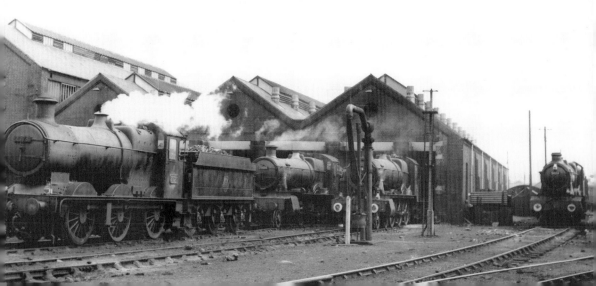

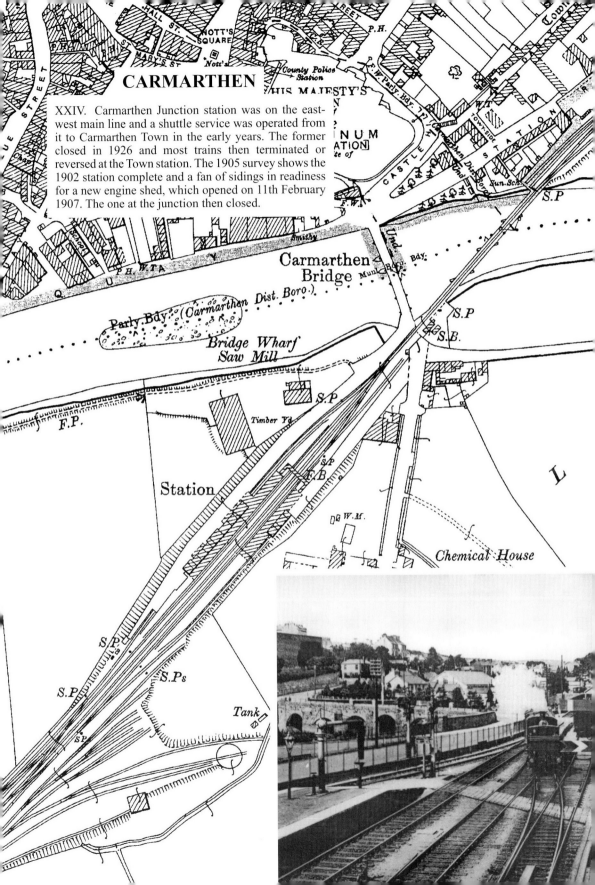

CARMARTHEN

XXIV. Carmarthen Junction station was on the east-west main line and a shuttle service was operated from it to Carmarthen Town in the early years. The former closed in 1926 and most trains then terminated or reversed at the Town station. The 1905 survey shows the 1902 station complete and a fan of sidings in readiness for a new engine shed, which opened on 11th February 1907. The one at the junction then closed.

66.   The goods shed is in the background as 0-6-0PT no. 7422 runs south sometime in 1959. On the left is Carmarthen Crossing Box, which had 58 levers and was in use from 15th August 1931 until 15th December 1968. (D.K.Jones coll.)

67. The 11.55am from Aberystwyth crosses the Towy on 25th May 1963. The goods yard in the background closed to public traffic just prior to the signal box at the far end of it. Its 27-lever frame was in use until 13th July 1967. Goods traffic continued over the bridge until 1973. (E.Wilmshurst)

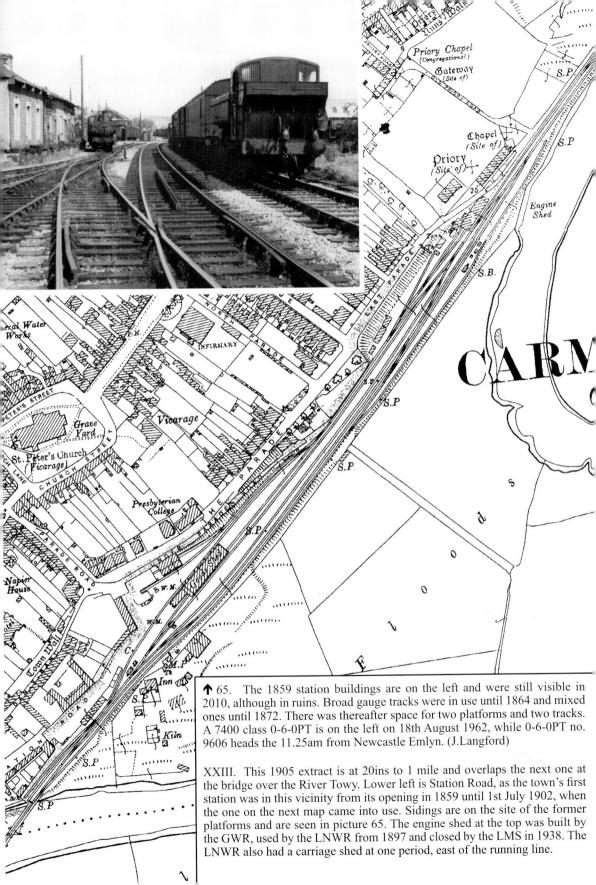

65. The 1859 station buildings are on the left and were still visible in 2010, although in ruins. Broad gauge tracks were in use until 1864 and mixed ones until 1872. There was thereafter space for two platforms and two tracks. A 7400 class 0-6-0PT is on the left on 18th August 1962, while 0-6-0PT no. 9606 heads the 11.25am from Newcastle Emlyn. (J.Langford)

XXIII. This 1905 extract is at 20ins to 1 mile and overlaps the next one at the bridge over the River Towy. Lower left is Station Road, as the town's first station was in this vicinity from its opening in 1859 until 1st July 1902, when the one on the next map came into use. Sidings are on the site of the former platforms and are seen in picture 65. The engine shed at the top was built by the GWR, used by the LNWR from 1897 and closed by the LMS in 1938. The LNWR also had a carriage shed at one period, east of the running line.

63.　　Looking in the other direction in 1956, we see the sharp bend in the road at the yard entrance. Goods traffic ceased on 2nd December 1963. The signal box had a 23-lever frame and was in use from 1893 to 1965. (H.C.Casserley)

NORTH OF CARMARTHEN

64.　　One mile north of the present Carmarthen station was Abergwili Junction, where a line branched east to Llandilo from 1863 to 1964. The single track is behind the train, which is running from Aberystwyth to Carmarthen, sometime in the 1950s. The 41-lever signal box was in use from 1896 until 24th February 1964. Vans stand in front of it, on an exchange siding. (W.A.Camwell/SLS coll.)

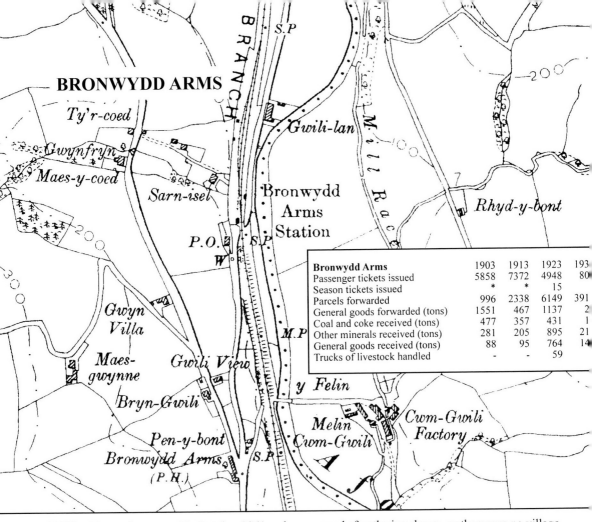

BRONWYDD ARMS

Ty'r-coed
Gwynfryn
Maes-y-coed
Sarn-isel
Gwili-lan
Bronwydd Arms Station
BRANCH
S.P
Mill Race
Rhyd-y-bont
P.O.
S.P
W
Gwyn Villa
Maes-gwynne
Gwili View
Bryn-Gwili
Pen-y-bont
Bronwydd Arms (P.H.)
M.P
y Felin
Melin Cwm-Gwili
Cwm-Gwili Factory
S.P

Bronwydd Arms	1903	1913	1923	193
Passenger tickets issued	5858	7372	4948	80
Season tickets issued	*	*	15	
Parcels forwarded	996	2338	6149	391
General goods forwarded (tons)	1551	467	1137	2
Coal and coke received (tons)	477	357	431	1
Other minerals received (tons)	281	205	895	21
General goods received (tons)	88	95	764	14
Trucks of livestock handled	-	-	59	

XXII.   The station opened in October 1861 and was named after the inn shown, as there was no village nearby. The map is from 1907 and is at 12ins to 1 mile.

62.   A look north in 1937 includes most of both of the goods loops. There were two men recorded here in 1903-38. See pictures 111 onwards for the revival story. (Stations UK)

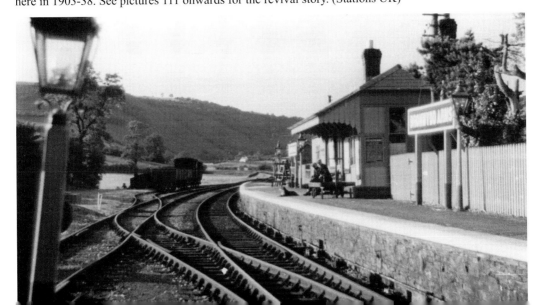

60.　　　Running in on 13th July 1956 is the 5.45pm from Aberystwyth, hauled by 2-6-0 no. 5353. The 1893 signal box had 15 levers and lasted until the end of passenger operation. (H.C.Casserley)

61.　　　The yard is seen on the same day. It closed on 2nd December 1963. Almost two miles to the south was Quarry Sidings, from about 1893 to 1906. (H.C.Casserley)

CONWIL

Map labels: F.B. · Dol-Gwili · Spout · Tank S.P. · Ford · Cwm-coy · W. S.B. · Conwil Station · Railway Hotel · Ty'r-Gwili · S.P. · M.P. · Spring · Lan- · 200 · 300 · 400 · 500

XXI. The station and the route southwards opened on 3rd September 1860, but the station closed in the period 31st December 1860 to 15th August 1861. The 1907 survey is at 12ins to 1 mile.

Conwil	1903	1913	1923	1933
Passenger tickets issued	9250	7739	1526	6151
Season tickets issued	*	*	44	-
Parcels forwarded	1355	1488	4206	2303
General goods forwarded (tons)	727	1155	287	242
Coal and coke received (tons)	2165	1095	1250	546
Other minerals received (tons)	2454	655	1313	1752
General goods received (tons)	913	1105	606	218
Trucks of livestock handled	46	100	150	149

59. Two trains are northbound sometime in the 1950s and we witness class 4300 2-6-0 no. 5306 overtaking no. 8103, a 2-6-2T of class 8100. There were two men employed here in 1903-38. (W.A.Camwell/SLS coll.)

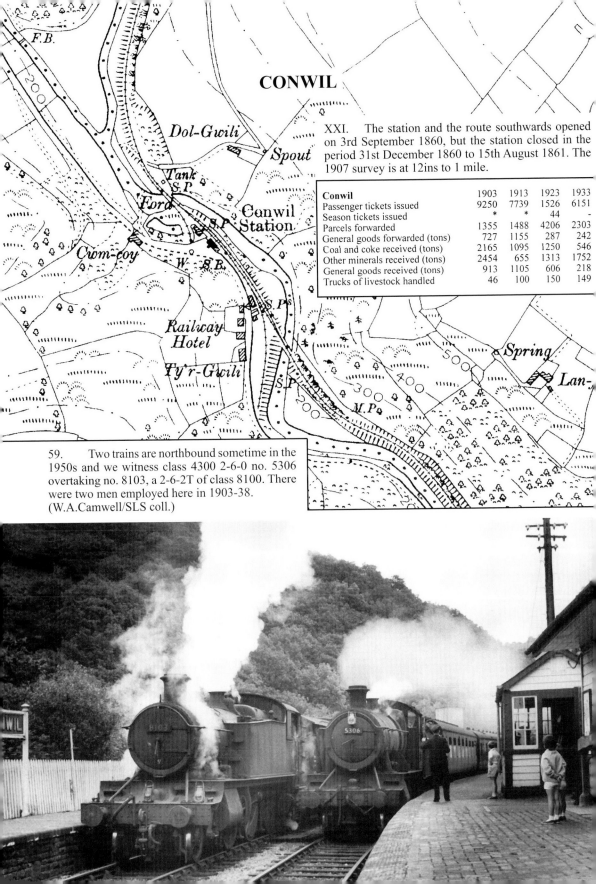

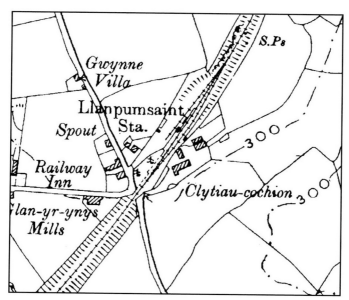

XX.   The village has one "p" in local use, but always two in railway publications. This is the 1948 survey at 12ins to 1 mile.

58.   An 0-6-0PT enters the idyllic scene in 1937, when there were just two employees. Goods traffic ceased on 2nd December 1963, but the 17-lever signal box functioned until 22nd February 1965, when passenger traffic ended. (Stations UK)

LLANPUMPSAINT

57.　　A southward panorama has the Railway Inn centre, on the side of the valley. The reason for short sidings is now obvious. The platform on the left was added in 1894. (Lens of Sutton coll.)

Llanpumpsaint	1903	1913	1923	1933
Passenger tickets issued	6530	7477	6217	2870
Season tickets issued	*	*	33	2
Parcels forwarded	1466	1319	1712	1590
General goods forwarded (tons)	85	1031	414	44
Coal and coke received (tons)	851	433	345	226
Other minerals received (tons)	523	268	500	345
General goods received (tons)	414	502	418	864
Trucks of livestock handled	5	-	11	6

55.   No. 6310 was a class 4300 2-6-0 and it waits to depart south in about 1956. The 35-lever frame was in use from September 1894 to July 1967. The goods yard had closed on 6th September 1965. (J.W.T.House/C.L.Caddy coll.)

56.   The prospective passenger's perspective was recorded on 9th July 1958, along with the Royal Mail van and the photographer's 1934 Hillman 10. Trains running south would pass through Pencader Tunnel (983yds) after two miles and then reach Pencader Tunnel Loop, which was in use from 1905 to 1935 and again briefly in 1937. Its box had 19 levers. (H.C.Casserley)

53.   A view south has the goods shed beyond the water tank and the engine shed beyond the locomotive. The latter shed closed on 2nd March 1918 and the nearby turntable was removed in 1927. (Chambers/HMRS)

54.   A view south from the footbridge in September 1952 includes the access to the goods yard and also the siding which earlier served the engine shed. There was once a siding to a chemical works in the left background. (H.C.Casserley)

51.   In the early years, northbound passengers had to change here from a GWR train to a M&MR one. The former used the platform next to the main building (right). M&MR stock is featured, including part of their 2-4-0 no. 3 *Lady Elizabeth*, seen fully in picture no. 1. (P.Q.Treloar coll.)

52.   Seen from the castle mound is the M&MR waiting room, with an equally well supported urinal. A small lane passes under the railway and over the river in this congested valley. The spacious GWR goods shed is in the right background. (Lens of Sutton coll.)

PENCADER

XIX.   The 1904 edition includes three woollen mills and a two-road engine shed, near the turntable. There was a staff of 13 in 1903-23, but only 8 in the 1930s.

Pencader	1903	1913	1923	1933
Passenger tickets issued	17202	22698	15506	4385
Season tickets issued	*	*	30	20
Parcels forwarded	3572	5295	5227	3434
General goods forwarded (tons)	1182	1930	1037	152
Coal and coke received (tons)	1027	1034	675	113
Other minerals received (tons)	394	665	453	1183
General goods received (tons)	1750	1788	1402	1043
Trucks of livestock handled	348	358	532	128

BRYN TEIFY

49.   A train departs north in the 1950s and gives passengers their first sight of an austere M&MR station building. The signal box was a late arrival, being completed in 1895, with a ten-lever frame. (W.A.Camwell/SLS coll.)

XVIII.   We use the name applied from October 1916, Cross Inn being a common precursor. New Quay Road was another, but there is much uncertainty, which we will not repeat. It seems that the station opened on 6th September 1869 and had two employees in 1913-38. The 12ins scale map is from 1948.

Bryn Teify	1913	1923	1933
Passenger tickets issued	6421	4666	1628
Season tickets issued	*	-	-
Parcels forwarded	2038	2765	3100
General goods forwarded (tons)	191	137	124
Coal and coke received (tons)	547	422	229
Other minerals received (tons)	169	229	192
General goods received (tons)	750	777	921
Trucks of livestock handled	947	1365	1218

NORTH OF PENCADER

50.   It is 18th August 1962 and we view a north-bound freight train from the brake van of a goods from Newcastle Emlyn. Pencader Junction is behind us and there had been a signal box there until 21st July 1929. The junction was then controlled from Pencader station box, until a ground frame was provided in November 1956. M&MR rails finished here. (J.Langford)

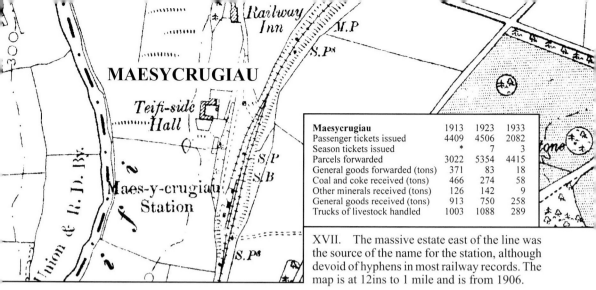

MAESYCRUGIAU

Maesycrugiau	1913	1923	1933
Passenger tickets issued	4409	4506	2082
Season tickets issued	*	7	3
Parcels forwarded	3022	5354	4415
General goods forwarded (tons)	371	83	18
Coal and coke received (tons)	466	274	58
Other minerals received (tons)	126	142	9
General goods received (tons)	913	750	258
Trucks of livestock handled	1003	1088	289

XVII. The massive estate east of the line was the source of the name for the station, although devoid of hyphens in most railway records. The map is at 12ins to 1 mile and is from 1906.

47. The M&MR provided its standard small building and this was supplemented by the GWR with a pair of its stylish Pagoda shelters. One siding runs behind the signal box, which had 12 levers and its dates are as for Llanybyther. (Stations UK)

48. A southward panorama in the 1960s completes the survey. There was a staff of two throughout the 1930s. Almost two miles to the south was Bryn Teify Tunnel, which was 101yds in length. It is shown on the next map. (Lens of Sutton coll.)

45.   The bridge replaced a level crossing at an unknown date and is seen moments after the previous picture was taken. The yard had a 3-ton crane. (R.M.Casserley)

46.   The 5.50pm Carmarthen to Aberystwyth is seen on 13th August 1963, behind 0-6-0 no. 2287. The siding on the left continued to the cattle dock. Goods traffic ceased on 6th September 1965 and the signal box closed on 22nd February 1965. (L.W.Rowe)

Llanybyther	1913	1923	1933
Passenger tickets issued	15029	17111	4139
Season tickets issued	*	46	8
Parcels forwarded	11991	11080	11906
General goods forwarded (tons)	1196	1135	545
Coal and coke received (tons)	2588	1394	1142
Other minerals received (tons)	1246	1966	1887
General goods received (tons)	4458	4889	3591
Trucks of livestock handled	6782	12409	7737

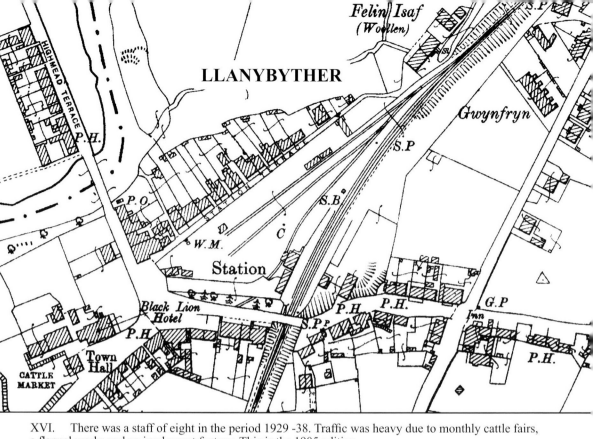

XVI.   There was a staff of eight in the period 1929 -38. Traffic was heavy due to monthly cattle fairs, a flannel works and an implement factory. This is the 1905 edition.

44.   Southbound on 7th July 1958 is 0-6-0 no. 2200. The signal box had 12 levers when completed in 1895. It was moved in 1908 onto a new brick base and a new frame of 15 levers installed. It is probable that the platforms were extended at the same time. (H.C.Casserley)

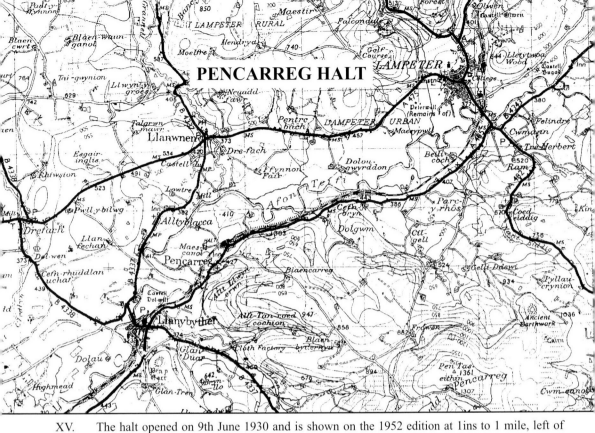

PENCARREG HALT

XV.   The halt opened on 9th June 1930 and is shown on the 1952 edition at 1ins to 1 mile, left of centre.

43.   We look towards Lampeter in about 1960. The halt served only a few dwellings, but was very conveniently situated to the lake. (Lens of Sutton coll.)

42.   The siding on the right served the cattle dock and was usable until January 1966. The main building was demolished in 1982, having been photographed in 1967 in the presence of a milk train. (T.David/C.L.Caddy coll.)

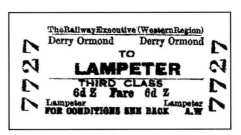

40.	Another southward view and this includes two trains waiting to depart, in about 1957. Public goods traffic continued until 22nd September 1973. (W.A.Camwell/SLS coll.)

41.	The signal box had 23 levers and was in use until 2nd January 1966. The signalman was able to supervise passengers who were using the barrow crossing. The main building was demolished and a cattle market was developed on part of the goods yard site. (Lens of Sutton coll.)

38.   The 1916 Dalis Fair outcome was well photographed, herding being illustrated graphically lower right. Tregaron would have witnessed similar scenes. Staff levels dropped from 12 to 9 in the period 1923-33. (Lens of Sutton coll.)

39.   Crowds gathered to witness the departure of the 9th Welch Regiment during World War I. Our view south includes the former signal box (right), which housed a ground frame from 17th May 1916, when the platforms were lengthened. (Lens of Sutton coll.)

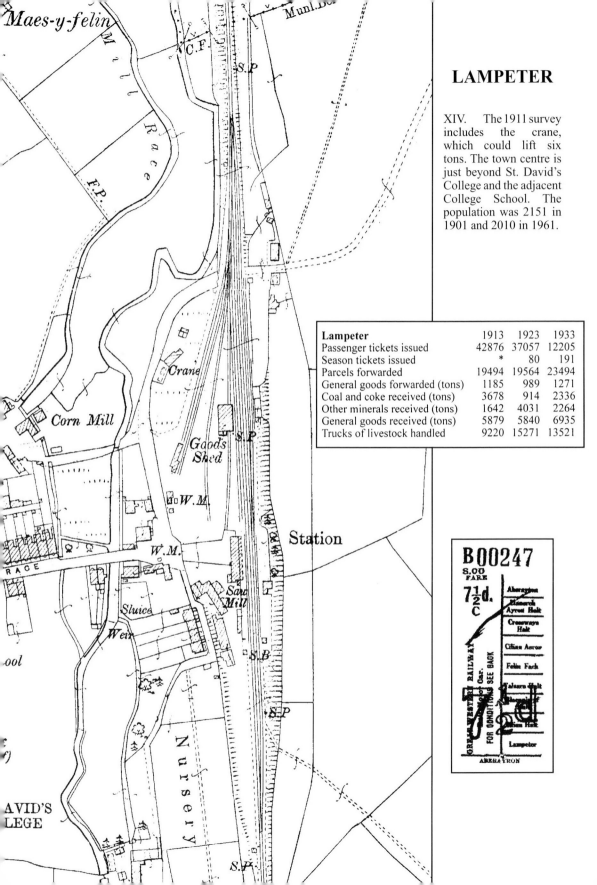

Maes-y-felin

LAMPETER

XIV. The 1911 survey includes the crane, which could lift six tons. The town centre is just beyond St. David's College and the adjacent College School. The population was 2151 in 1901 and 2010 in 1961.

Lampeter	1913	1923	1933
Passenger tickets issued	42876	37057	12205
Season tickets issued	*	80	191
Parcels forwarded	19494	19564	23494
General goods forwarded (tons)	1185	989	1271
Coal and coke received (tons)	3678	914	2336
Other minerals received (tons)	1642	4031	2264
General goods received (tons)	5879	5840	6935
Trucks of livestock handled	9220	15271	13521

Corn Mill

Crane

Goods Shed

W. M.

W. M.

Station

Saw Mill

Sluice

Weir

S.B

Nursery

AVID'S LEGE

B 00247

8.00 FARE

7½d. C

GREAT WESTERN RAILWAY

FOR CONDITIONS SEE BACK

Aberayron
Blaenech
Aylron Halt
Crossways Halt
Cilian Aeron
Felin Fach
Talsarn Halt
Silian Halt
Lampeter
ABERAYRON

36.　　　The goods yard closed on 2nd December 1963 and the 9-lever signal box followed on 22nd February 1965. Behind the box is the coal store, but the stove chimney is below ridge level. (P.J.Garland/R.S.Carpenter coll.)

NORTH OF LAMPETER

37.　　　A northward view of Aberayron Junction in July 1958 has the Aberayron branch on the left. The signal box site was to the right of the camera. It had 12 levers and closed on 21st August 1929. (H.C.Casserley)

DERRY ORMOND

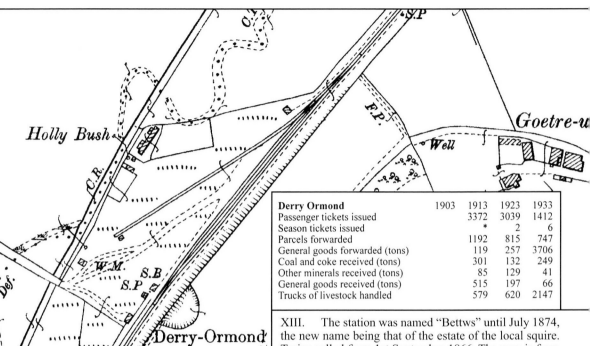

Derry Ormond	1903	1913	1923	1933
Passenger tickets issued		3372	3039	1412
Season tickets issued		*	2	6
Parcels forwarded		1192	815	747
General goods forwarded (tons)		119	257	3706
Coal and coke received (tons)		301	132	249
Other minerals received (tons)		85	129	41
General goods received (tons)		515	197	66
Trucks of livestock handled		579	620	2147

XIII. The station was named "Bettws" until July 1874, the new name being that of the estate of the local squire. Trains called from 1st September 1866. The map is from 1905.

35. The well kept station was photographed on 15th July 1961. It had a staff of two between 1929 and 1938. Here was the luxury of two fires or stoves. (A.M.Davies)

LLANGYBI

XII.   It seems that the station came into use sometime in 1869, but trains only stopped on the market days of Lampeter and Tregaron. Mondays were added later and from 1875, most trains would stop. The map is from 1948 and is at 6ins to 1 mile.

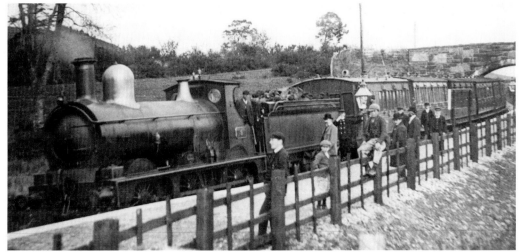

33.   M&MR no. 9 was on hire from the GWR in 1905 and was one of the "Dean Goods" 0-6-0s built at its Swindon Works. Substantial trains were operated to local fairs and for the pleasure of a visit to Aberystwyth. (P.Q.Treloar coll.)

34.   The other road bridge is featured in this 1960s view. The lamp was to help locate the stop. Staffing ceased here on 28th November 1947; the 1938 listing showed the station accepting passengers and horse boxes only. There were 8054 tickets issued in 1923, but only 382 in 1936. (Lens of Sutton coll.)

XI.   The 1952 edition at 1 ins to 1 mile has the halt near its centre. The branch to Aberayron is on the left.

31.   This is the "Milk Branches Rail Tour" on 12th September 1970. It started at Cardiff at 09.45, returning at 19.30. It is seen again in picture 110 and was operated jointly by the Wirral Railway Circle and the Branch Line Society. (M.Dart)

OLMARCH HALT

32.   Opening took place on 7th December 1929 and the stop was just over two miles from Pont Llanio. It was near the head of the Dulas Valley, at over 500ft above sea level. (Lens of Sutton coll.)

29.   It is July 1957 and 2-6-0 no. 6310 stops its train from Aberystwyth at a point convenient for milk churns, rather than passengers. There was a staff of two in the 1930s. The other signals can be seen in the front cover photograph. (J.W.T.House/C.L.Caddy coll.)

30.   A June 1965 record shows the depot at its optimum, closure coming in 1969. General freight ceased on 16th April 1964, but the line south to Aberayron Junction was open for milk traffic until 1st October 1970. (P.J.Garland/R.S.Carpenter coll.)

PONT LLANIO

28.　　A panorama from the road bridge in 1937 includes the Milk Marketing Board's premises under construction. The small signal box, housing 8 levers, was moved from the far end of the platform to the position shown in 1895 to meet new sighting rules. It also enabled the loop to be extended at the Aberystwyth end in 1910. It closed on 22nd February 1965. The crane (centre) was rated at 2½ tons. (Stations UK)

Pont Llanio	1913	1923	1933
Passenger tickets issued	14182	10297	3207
Season tickets issued	*	11	19
Parcels forwarded	3199	3284	2308
General goods forwarded (tons)	283	257	231
Coal and coke received (tons)	593	208	555
Other minerals received (tons)	516	418	605
General goods received (tons)	1464	805	457
Trucks of livestock handled	1850	2194	1379

X. Scaled at 12ins to 1 mile, this 1948 map has the revised track layout.

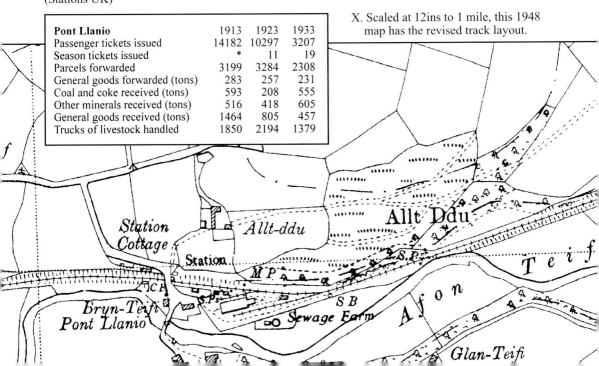

26.   The size of the goods shed reflects the volume of traffic. There were 6 or 7 employees here in the 1920-38 period. The 24-lever signal box was in use from 1909 until 22nd February 1965. The goods yard closed on 16th March 1964; there had been a one-ton crane in the shed.
(P.J.Garland/R.S.Carpenter coll.)

27.   Here is the north end of the loop in 1965, together with the cottage for the crossing keeper. The road was numbered A485 in 1919. (P.J.Garland/R.S.Carpenter coll.)

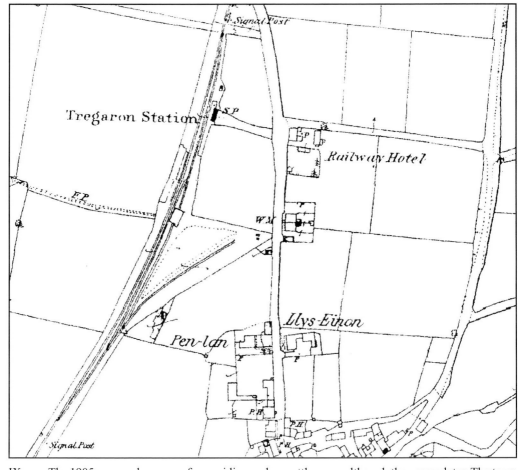

IX.   The 1905 survey shows one fewer siding and no cattle pens, although they came later. The town was noted for its fairs and horse dealing. The tiny signal box is just north of the main building, which is infilled in black.

25.   This is the north end of the loop on 17th June 1963, as the 10.35am from Carmarthen pulls in behind 2-6-4T no. 80105. The lamp room is on the left. (H.C.Casserley)

TREGARON

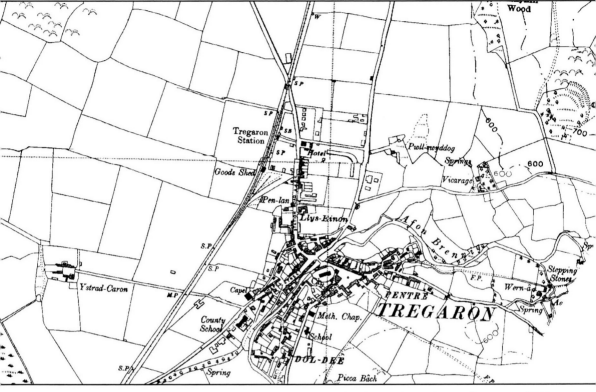

VIII.   The 1948 edition at 6ins to 1 mile reveals the relationship of the station to the town, which housed 1509 souls in 1901.

24.   M&MR stock and architecture are featured in this view of its no. 5, an 0-6-0 built by Sharp Stewart in 1870. The GWR withdrew it in 1906. (P.Q.Treloar coll.)

ALLTDDU HALT

23.   This stop came into use on 23rd September 1935. Approaching on 17th June 1963 is 4-6-0 no. 7826 *Longworth Manor* with the 11.55am from Aberystwyth to Carmarthen. The great wilderness of the red bog is included; it is a paradise for ornithologists. (R.M.Casserley)

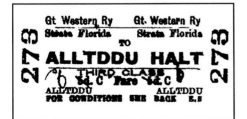

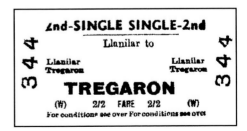

← 20. Looking in the other direction in 1958, we see the entire provision for passengers. In the distance is the massive area of bog. The ruins of the abbey, after which the station was named, were 2½ miles to the east. (D.K.Jones coll.)

← 21. The middle building was for goods and parcels. The signal box was built in 1895 and had 12 levers. It closed on 22nd February 1965, when the station ceased to act as a temporary terminus and the route to Carmarthen lost all passenger trains. (W.A.Camwell/SLS coll.)

22. The 11.55am from Aberystwyth was hauled by 2-6-0 no. 6310 on 9th June 1960. On the left is the 10.35 from Carmarthen, while a class 2251 0-6-0 stands on the line which was to have carried trains to Manchester. The goods yard had a 3-ton crane and closed on 16th April 1964. (H.Ballantyne)

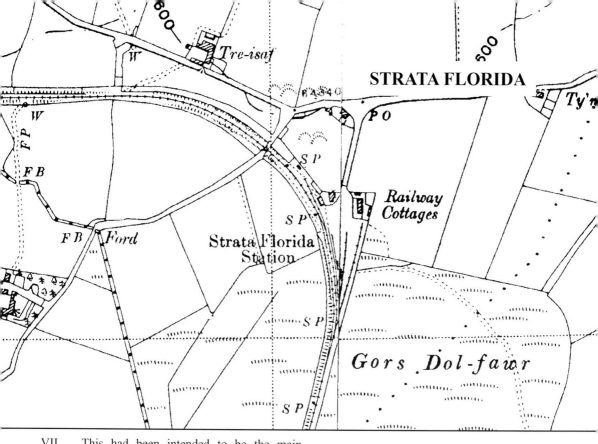

VII. This had been intended to be the main junction on the M&MR, with the line to Llanidloes continuing north from the straight section on the right. This is the 1948 edition at 12ins to 1 mile.

19. A northward panorama from 1937 includes the cattle pens below the water tank. The latter was used by most northbound trains, as a severe climb of over one mile started near to it. The house in the centre was for the station master; he had two men to supervise in the 1930s. (Stations UK)

Strata Florida	1913	1923	1933
Passenger tickets issued	12553	13310	6354
Season tickets issued	*	10	15
Parcels forwarded	3495	2443	2159
General goods forwarded (tons)	1429	330	105
Coal and coke received (tons)	530	596	409
Other minerals received (tons)	390	317	385
General goods received (tons)	1473	1077	797
Trucks of livestock handled	2422	2522	1775

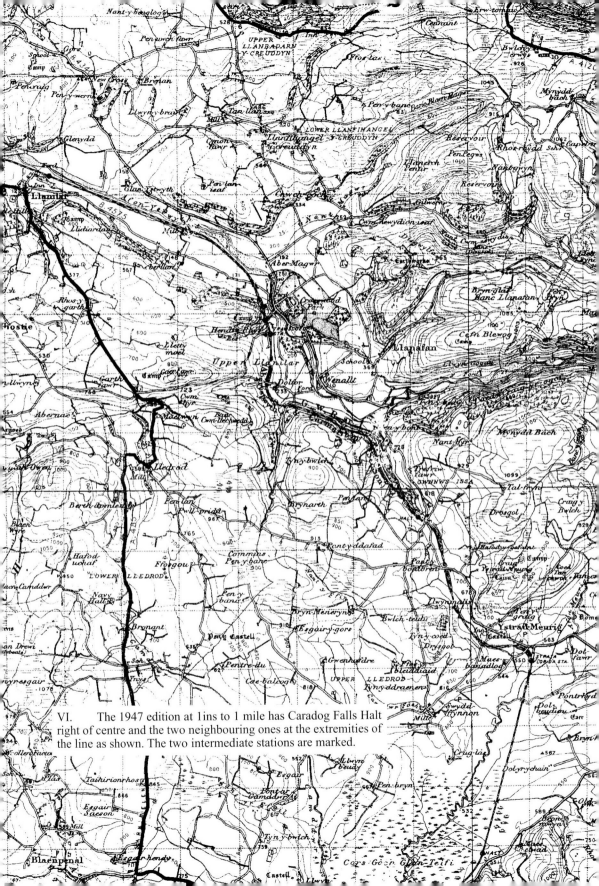

VI.   The 1947 edition at 1ins to 1 mile has Caradog Falls Halt right of centre and the two neighbouring ones at the extremities of the line as shown. The two intermediate stations are marked.

CARADOG FALLS HALT

18.   We are on the same train as seen in picture 16 and in the distance is the 86yd long Tynygraig Tunnel, which is at the watershed between the Ystwyth and Teifi valleys. The halt opened on 5th September 1932, mainly in the interest of tourism. One mile to the south, there was a siding on the east side of the line for Ystrad Meurig Quarry, from 1894 to 1954. It produced mainly roadstone and was owned by Aberystwyth Corporation. (P.J.Garland/R.S.Carpenter coll.)

17.   The two sidings were in front of the signal box and were in use until 12th December 1963. This photograph is from June 1965, by which time the coal arrived by road. There was a single siding behind the box from 1917 for a timber firm. (P.J.Garland/R.S.Carpenter coll.)

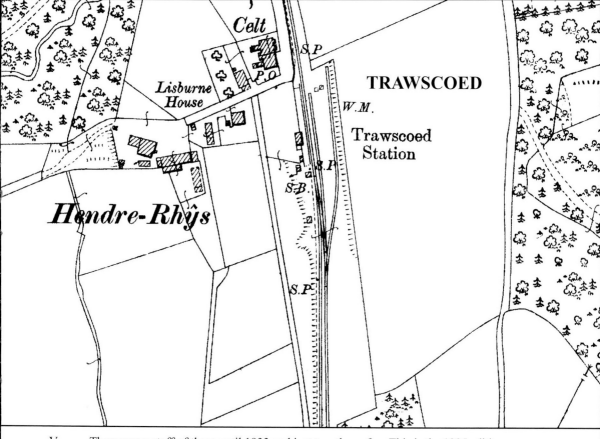

Celt

Lisburne
House

P.O

S P

TRAWSCOED

W.M.

Trawscoed
Station

Hendre-Rhŷs

S.P

S.B

S.P

V.   There was a staff of three until 1933 and just two thereafter. This is the 1905 edition.

16.   We are on a southbound train on 22nd March 1962. The signal box had 11 levers and closed on
22nd February 1965. One chimney had to suffice for the entire station.
(P.J.Garland/R.S.Carpenter coll.)

FELINDYFFRYN HALT

15.   The halt came into use on 10th June 1935 and seems to have had less than ten houses within a mile of it. This 1960s view includes modernisation in the form of a bracket from which to hang a pressurised Tilley oil lamp. The milepost reads 33¾. (Lens of Sutton coll.)

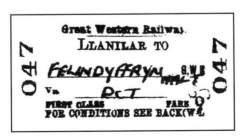

13.　　The platform on the left had been added in 1907 and the loop was further lengthened in 1917. On the left is the isolated facility for gentlemen. (W.A.Camwell/SLS coll.)

14.　　A Hymek diesel is seen with the 11.55 Aberystwyth to Carmarthen in the last year of operation. The signal box had 14 levers and closed on 22nd February 1965. (J.W.T.House/C.L.Caddy coll.)

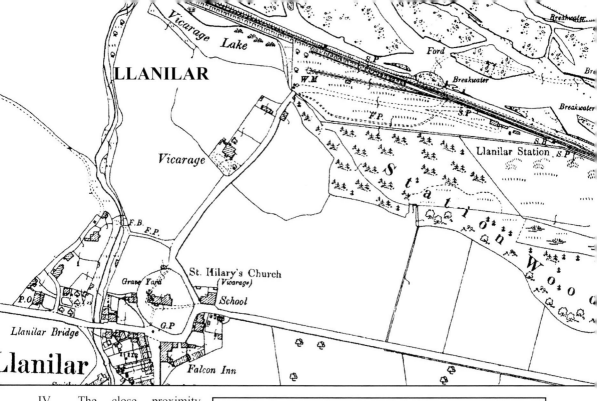

IV. The close proximity of the Afon Ystwyth is evident on this 1905 extract at 6ins to 1 mile. It was the destruction of the railway by floods in this vicinity that brought about its premature closure. The signal box was moved away from the track in 1907 and a new frame of 14 levers was installed.

Llanilar	1903	1913	1923	1933
Passenger tickets issued		10750	9978	4093
Season tickets issued		*	30	32
Parcels forwarded		1199	1117	895
General goods forwarded (tons)		25	168	19
Coal and coke received (tons)		177	501	158
Other minerals received (tons)		285	728	1140
General goods received (tons)		351	439	203
Trucks of livestock handled		425	1426	722

12. A view west in 1937 features clean lanterns ready to receive paraffin lamps at dusk. There were two men employed at that time. In the distance is the goods yard, which closed on 2nd December 1963. It had a 30cwt crane. (Stations UK)

11. The much larger GWR box contained only 17 levers and lasted to the end, but was reduced to a ground frame in 1931. Seen in 1937, the goods yard was in use until 2nd December 1963. There was a staff of two in the 1920s and one in the 1930s. (Stations UK)

Llanrhystyd Road	1903	1913	1923	1933
Passenger tickets issued		11819	12309	1482
Season tickets issued		*	51	6
Parcels forwarded		1054	663	344
General goods forwarded (tons)		37	184	14
Coal and coke received (tons)		438	500	442
Other minerals received (tons)		230	688	1349
General goods received (tons)		194	253	100
Trucks of livestock handled		491	1397	1083

255 255
3rd-SINGLE   SINGLE-3rd
Aberystwyth to
Aberystwyth   Aberystwyth
Llanrhystyd Road   Llanrhystyd Road
LLANRHYSTYD ROAD
(W)   6d H   FARE   6d H (W)
For Conditions see over For Conditions see over
255 255

Manchester & Milford Railway.
LLANILAR
TO
LLANYBYTHER
First Class.
143

LLANRHYSTYD ROAD

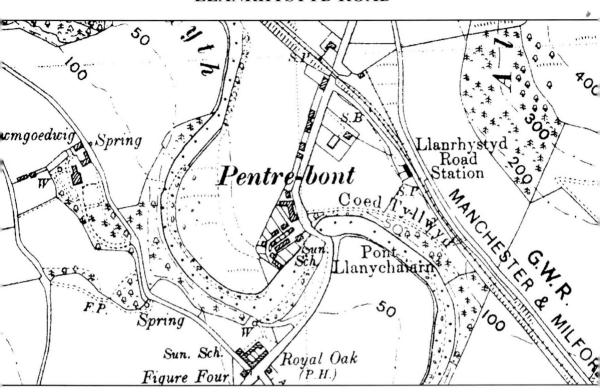

III.   The station is about 100ft above sea level, but the route from Aberystwyth climbed to a greater height before descending at 1 in 66 to this stop. This is the 1938 edition at 12ins to 1 mile.

10.   This view contains entirely M&MR structures, the signal box lasting until January 1912. Llanrhystyd was six miles distant. The loop and platform were both lengthened in November 1911. (Lens of Sutton coll.)

8. A panorama from 1st June 1979 shows that the area between the tracks served as the platform for Devils Bridge passengers from 1968. The canopies had been removed in 1969. Ready to leave is 2-6-2T no. 8 *Llewellyn*. (T.Heavyside)

9. The engine shed has been coded 89C and closed on 10th April 1965. It reopened for VofR stock on 20th May 1968 and it is seen on 9th August 1987, with no. 7 *Owain Glyndwr* at the west end. (D.H.Mitchell)

7.   Our final view from 1962 features the 100-lever signal box, which was in use until 24th April 1982. The goods yard also closed that day. (C.C.Green/G.Williams coll.)

Other views of this station can be found in the companion albums *Newtown to Aberystwyth* (pictures 112 to 120) and *Corris and Vale of Rheidol* (pictures 61 to 91).

6.   The GWR operated all services from 1922 and rebuilt the station very extensively in a neo-Georgian style, completion being in 1926. The concourse is seen in 1962, along with the three ticket office windows. The structures were still complete almost 50 years later, but concerned with catering. (C.C.Green/G.Williams coll.)

4.   Waiting to depart for Carmarthen on 24th June 1954 is 2-6-0 no. 6310. The terminus for VofR trains was behind the fence on the left from 1925 until 1967. Trains from Carmarthen commonly arrived on the right from where the engine could be easily released. (R.F.Roberts/SLS coll.)

5.   Looking northeast in 1962, we have the high-level coal stage under the water tank on the right, the engine shed (plus repair shop) in the centre and the M&MR's main premises on the left. Tank wagons in this picture, also no 7, are a reminder that diesel locomotives had recently been introduced here. (C.C.Green/G.Williams coll.)

2.   A poor postcard from the CR period is included as it looks towards the terminus from that company's engine approach. The layout and sheds were unchanged from 1906 until 1938; a turning triangle was added in 1940. (Lens of Sutton coll.)

3.   The 3.20 from Carmarthen arrives behind ex-GWR 4-4-0 no. 9013 on 24th June 1953. On the right is the ex-M&MR works. (R.J.Buckley/P.Q.Treloar coll.)

1. Aberystwyth to Carmarthen

ABERYSTWYTH

ABERYSTWYTH

II.   The 1938 survey at 6ins to 1 mile has the Carmarthen route lower left, with the Afon Rheidol and the Vale of Rheidol line passing under it. The latter ends between the main station and its car park. The former passes the QUAY before reaching the sea. The VofR had a track to it in the early years. Similarly, the M&MR had a line to the wharf on the other side of the river in part of the 19th century. Some of the earthwork can be seen south of the Isolation Hospital. A trailing branch ran over a bridge to the PIER. The triangular building at the south end of Park Avenue had earlier been the engineering works and foundry of the M&MR.

1.   GWR locomotives were soon predominant south hereof, after its takeover of the M&MR. This is a rare view of one of the latter's locomotives, in 1906. It is no. 3 *Lady Elizabeth*, which was built by Sharp Stewart in 1866. The M&MR had six other engines by 1906. (P.Q.Treloar coll.)

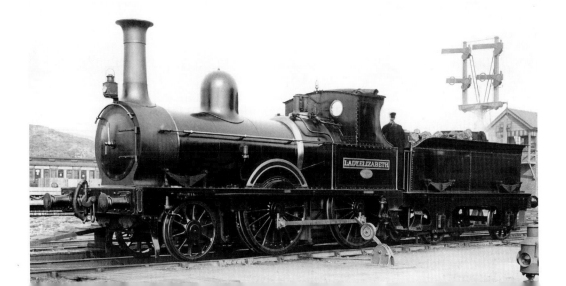

October 1912

CARMARTHEN, NEWCASTLE EMLYN, and ABERYSTWYTH.

Mls. frm Cmrthn	Down.	Week Days only. aft	mrn	mrn	mrn	aft	mrn	aft
	Paddington Station, 60 London ....dep.	9 15	1 c 0	..	8 45	..	1130	..
	Carmarthen ....dep.	5 30	10 5	..	1 35	2 20	5 8	7 10
3¼	Bronwydd Arms	5 40	1015	..	..	2 30	5 18	7 20
6¾	Conwil	5 49	1024	..	..	2 39	5 28	7 32
9½	Llanpumpsaint	5 57	1033	..	..	2 49	5 40	7 42
14½	Pencader ....arr.	6 15	1048	..	..	3 2	5 55	7 55
—	Pencader ....dep.	6 20	1055	1135	..	3 17	6 5	8 5
18	Llandyssil	6 28	11 8	1144	..	3 29	6 17	8 15
19¾	Pentrecourt Platform	6 33	1112	1149	..	3 33	6 21	Saturdays only.
22	Henllan	6 40	1118	1156	..	3 40	6 28	
25	Newcastle Emlyn ....arr.	6 48	1125	12 5	..	3 48	6 35	
—	Pencader ....dep.	6 40	1050	..	..	3 10	6 0	
16½	New Quay Road	6 47	1055	..	..	3 17	6 5	
18¾	Maesycrugiau	6 51	11 4	..	..	3 21	6 10	
22¾	Llanybyther	7 4	1113	..	..	3 32	6 20	
27½	Lampeter 79 ....arr.	7 17	1127	..	2 38	3 41	6 30	
	dep.	7 22	1132	..	2 41	3 45	6 35	
29¾	Derry Ormond	7 28	1138	..	..	3 51	6 40	..
30¾	Llangybi	7 32	1142	..	..	3 55	6 45	..
34¾	Pont Llanio	7 40	1150	..	..	4 3	6 52	..
37	Tregaron	7 47	1157	..	..	4 8	7 0	..
42	Strata Florida	8 2	12 8	..	..	4 20	7 10	..
47	Trawscoed	8 16	1222	..	..	4 34	7 25	..
50	Llanilar	8 22	1229	..	..	4 41	7 30	..
53	Llanrhystyd Road	8 28	1235	..	..	4 50	7 38	..
56	Aberystwyth 477 ....arr.	8 40	1247	..	3 40	4 55	7 45	..

Miles	Up.	Week Days only. mrn	mrn	aft	aft	aft	aft
	Aberystwyth ....dep.	7 0	9 35	..	1 5	3 10	6 10
3	Llanrhystyd Road	7 8	9 43	..	1 13	3 18	6 18
6	Llanilar	7 15	9 50	..	1 20	3 25	6 24
9	Trawscoed	7 23	9 58	..	1 28	3 38	6 30
14	Strata Florida	7 39	1014	..	1 44	3 55	6 46
19	Tregaron	7 48	1024	..	1 54	4 10	6 55
21½	Pont Llanio	7 55	1030	..	2 0	4 18	7 5
25½	Llangybi	8 3	1038	..	2 8	4 25	7 15
26½	Derry Ormond	8 7	..	..	2 12	4 32	7 20
28½	Lampeter 79 ....arr.	8 12	1045	..	2 17	4 37	7 25
	dep.	8 15	1048	..	2 19	4 40	7 30
33½	Llanybyther	8 25	1058	..	2 28	4 52	7 38
37¼	Maesycrugiau	8 33	11 5	..	2 42	5 0	7 45
39½	New Quay Road	8 38	1116	..	2 50	5 7	7 53
41½	Pencader (above) ....arr.	8 43	1121	..	2 55	5 15	8 0
—	Mls Newcastle Emlyn ....dep.	8 10	1043	2 10	..	4 50	7 15
—	3 Henllan	8 18	1052	2 19	..	4 58	7 23
—	5½ Pentrecourt Platform	8 25	1059	2 25	..	5 5	7 35
—	7 Llandyssil	8 30	11 7	2 34	..	5 12	7 40
—	10½ Pencader (above) ....arr.	8 38	1117	2 42	..	5 23	7 49
—	Pencader ....dep.	8 49	1127	..	3 4	5 25	8 3
46½	Llanpumpsaint	9 3	1142	..	3 18	5 40	8 15
49½	Conwil	9 11	1153	..	3 26	5 50	8 23
52½	Bronwydd Arms ....[442	9 20	12 8	..	3 37	6 5	8 35
56	Carmarthen 60, 64. arr.	9 35	1220	..	3 46	6 15	8 45
276¾	64 London (Pad.) ....arr.	4 20	6 10	..	9 35	3 30	..

November 1930

CARMARTHEN, PENCADER, NEWCASTLE EMLYN, and ABERYSTWYTH.

Mls frm Cmrthn	Down.	Week Days. aft	mrn	mrn	mrn (Mondays only.)	mrn	mrn	mrn	aft (Except Saturdays. During School Vacation periods will run on Tuesdays and Fridays only.)	mrn	aft (Thursdays and Saturdays.)	Sundays. aft (Monday mornings.)
	62 London (Paddington) dep	9 25	..	..	..	12F55	..	8 55	..	1155	..	9 25
	Carmarthen ....dep.	5 30	..	..	..	10 0	..	2 20	..	6 5	..	5 30
3¼	Bronwydd Arms	5 40	..	..	..	10 10	..	2 30	..	6 16	..	5 40
6¾	Conwil	5 49	..	..	..	10 19	..	2 39	..	6 26	..	5 49
9½	Llanpumpsaint	5 59	..	..	..	10 27	..	2 47	..	6 35	..	5 59
14¼	Pencader ....arr.	6 10	..	..	..	10 40	..	3 3	..	6 50	..	6 10
—	Pencader ....dep.	..	6 20	8 55	..	10 50	1155	3 15	4 50	7 10	..	6 20
18½	Llandyssul A	..	6 29	9 4	..	10 59	12 4	3 24	5 0	7 19	..	6 29
20	Pentrecourt Platform	..	6 34	9 9	..	11 4	12 9	3 29	5 5	7 24	..	6 34
22¾	Henllan	..	6 41	9 16	..	11 13	1216	3 36	5 12	7 31	..	6 41
25	Newcastle Emlyn ....arr.	..	6 48	9 23	..	11 20	1224	3 43	5 19	7 38	..	6 48
—	Pencader ....dep.	6 23	..	..	..	10 45	..	3 7	..	7 2	..	6 23
16¾	Bryn Teify	6 28	..	..	..	10 51	..	3 12	..	7 7	..	6 28
18¾	Maesycrugiau	6 33	..	..	..	10 55	..	3 17	..	7 12	..	6 33
22¾	Llanybyther ¶	6 41	..	..	..	11 4	..	3 25	..	7 20	..	6 41
27½	Lampeter (below) ....arr.	6 53	..	..	..	11 16	..	3 37	..	7 33	..	6 53
	dep.	6 58	..	..	..	11 20	..	3 42	..	7 36	..	6 58
29¾	Derry Ormond	7 4	..	..	..	11 26	..	3 48	..	7 42	..	7 4
30¾	Llangybi ¶	7 8	..	..	..	11 30	..	3 52	..	7 46	..	7 8
34¾	Pont Llanio	7 17	..	..	..	11 40	..	4 2	..	7 56	..	7 17
37½	Tregaron	7 23	..	..	9 5	11 46	..	4 8	..	8 4	10 5	7 23
42½	Strata Florida	7 31	..	..	9 14	11 55	..	4 17	..	8 13	1014	7 31
47½	Trawscoed	7 50	..	..	9 29	12 10	..	4 32	..	8 28	1029	7 50
50½	Llanilar	7 57	..	..	9 36	12 16	..	4 39	..	8 34	1035	7 57
53½	Llanrhystyd Road	8 4	..	..	9 43	12 23	..	4 45	..	8 41	1042	8 4
56	Aberystwyth 138, 143 arr.	8 10	..	..	9 50	12 30	..	4 50	..	8 48	1050	8 10

Miles	Up.	Week Days. mrn	mrn	mrn	mrn	aft	aft (Except Saturdays. During School Vacation periods will run on Tuesdays and Fridays only.)	aft	aft (Mondays only.)	aft (Thursdays and Saturdays.)	Sundays.
	Aberystwyth ....dep.	..	6 50	..	9 55	1255	..	5 10	7 0	9 0	..
2¼	Llanrhystyd Road	..	7 1	..	10 3	1 3	..	5 18	7 8	9 8	..
5¼	Llanilar	..	7 8	..	1010	1 10	..	5 25	7 16	9 15	..
8½	Trawscoed	..	7 15	..	1017	1 17	..	5 32	7 24	9 22	..
13½	Strata Florida	..	7 33	..	1035	1 36	..	5 50	7 43	9 41	..
18½	Tregaron	..	7 44	..	1047	1 45	..	6 1	7 52	9 50	..
21¼	Pont Llanio ¶	..	7 50	..	1053	1 52	..	6 7	..	..	..
25¼	Llangybi	..	7 59	..	11 2	2 1	..	6 16	..	..	..
26¼	Derry Ormond	..	8 3	..	11 5	2 4	..	6 19	..	..	..
28½	Lampeter (below) ¶ ....arr.	..	8 8	..	1112	2 12	..	6 26	..	..	..
	dep.	..	8 12	..	1117	2 16	..	6 29	..	..	..
33½	Lanybyther	..	8 24	..	1129	2 28	..	6 40	..	..	..
37¼	Maesycrugiau	..	8 33	..	1137	2 36	..	6 49	..	..	..
39½	Bryn Teify	..	8 40	..	1142	2 41	..	6 56	..	..	..
41½	Pencader ....arr.	..	8 45	..	1147	2 45	..	7 1	..	..	..
—	Mls Newcastle Emlyn ....dep.	5 35	8 5	1010	11 5	2 5	4 10	6 15	..	..	..
—	3 Henllan	5 43	8 14	1018	1114	2 14	4 19	6 24	..	..	..
—	5½ Pentrecourt Platform	5 50	8 21	1025	1121	2 21	4 26	6 31	..	..	..
—	7 Llandyssul A	5 55	8 27	1030	1126	2 27	4 32	6 37	..	..	..
—	10½ Pencader ....arr.	6 3	8 35	1038	1134	2 35	4 40	6 45	..	..	..
—	Pencader ....dep.	..	8 49	..	1151	2 49	..	7 5	..	..	..
46½	Llanpumpsaint	..	9 3	..	12 5	3 5	..	7 19	..	..	..
49½	Conwil	..	9 11	..	1213	3 13	..	7 27	..	..	..
52½	Bronwydd Arms ....[513	..	9 23	..	1223	3 23	..	7 37	..	..	..
56	Carmarthen 62, 67, arr.	..	9 32	..	1232	3 32	..	7 46	..	..	..
276½	67 London (Pad.) ....arr.	..	3 10	..	6 10	9 40	..	3 30	..	..	..

A Station for New Quay (16 miles). F Except Mondays.

¶ "Halt" at Pencarreg between Llanybyther and Lampeter, and at Olmarch between Llangybi and Pont Llanio.

☞ A Service of Road Motors runs between Llandyssul Station and New Quay.

LAMPETER and ABERAYRON (Rail Auto-cars—One class only).

Miles		Week Days only. mrn	mrn	aft	aft
	Lampeter ¶ ....dep.	8 15	1130	3 50	7 40
7¼	Felin Fach ¶	8 42	1157	4 17	8 8
13¼	Aberayron C ....arr.	9 6	1222	4 41	8 33

Miles		Week Days only. mrn	mrn	aft	aft
	Aberayron ¶ ....dep.	7 5	10 0	1 10	5 20
6¼	Felin Fach ¶	7 28	1023	1 34	5 44
13¼	Lampeter (above) ....arr.	7 57	1052	2 3	6 13

C Station for New Quay (Cardigan Bay)—7¼ miles.

¶ "Halts" at Silian, at Blaenplwyf, and at Talsarn, between Lampeter and Felin Fach; at Ciliau-Aeron, at Crossways, and at Llanerch-Ayron, between Felin Fach and Aberayron.

PASSENGER SERVICES

Aberystwyth to Carmarthen

The early M&MR timetables offered three or four trains, weekdays only. There were no Sunday journeys on any of the routes, except one in the early hours, which provided a connection at Carmarthen.

Most passengers had to change at Pencader, although the GWR did operate a few through trains from Paddington and/or South Wales from 1902, for the holiday traffic. The route south of Pencader generally had a similar number of trains.

In most years between the wars, there were four services, but subsequently only three.

Aberayron Branch

In general, the service frequency was similar to that on the main line, but there were often some extras on Saturdays. There was an afternoon school trip between Felin Fach and Aberayron for many years in the 1930s.

Newcastle Emlyn Branch

During the period to 1895 when Llandyssul was the terminus, the number of trains was mostly the same as the main line. However, there was an increase subsequently, with five being a common figure, but seven appeared in some timetables in the 1930s.

June 1889

MANCHESTER & MILFORD [Traff. Man., E. Hamer.]

July 1896

PENCADER, LAMPETER, and ABERYSTWYTH.—Manchester and Milford.

July 1896

CARMARTHEN & CARDIGAN.—Great Western.

HISTORICAL BACKGROUND

The South Wales Railway reached Carmarthen from Swansea in 1852. It was broad gauge (7ft 0¼ins) and terminated south of the county town. It was extended west to Haverfordwest in 1854 and north to a station east of Carmarthen town centre in 1859. The routes became part of the Great Western Railway in 1863 and standard gauge in 1872.

The Carmarthen & Cardigan Railway was formed in 1854 and it opened north to Conwil on 3rd September 1860, using broad gauge track. It was closed from 31st December of that year until 15th August 1861. The route was extended to Pencader on 28th March 1864 and on to Llandyssul (on the Newcastle Emlyn branch) on 3rd June of that year.

A line east of Carmarthen from Llandeilo came into use with standard gauge track also in 1864. Thus there was mixed gauge track for about one mile, until the C&CR was converted to standard in 1866. The branch never reached Cardigan.

The Manchester & Milford Railway was created in 1854 to establish a fresh link between the cotton industries of Lancashire and the Atlantic ships. The monopoly of Liverpool was a problem and Milford Haven offered many advantages. The proposals included a branch to Aberystwyth for holiday traffic. The story of the problems and failures is long and complex. However, the Pencader-Lampeter section opened on 1st June 1866, the extension to Strata Florida came into use on 1st September 1866 and the link to Aberystwyth followed on 12th August 1867. Work started south of Llanidloes and is detailed in map XXV in *Brecon to Newtown*. A third rail was provided south of Pencader, so that M&MR trains could run over the C&CR to Carmarthen, but they were not allowed to call at intermediate stations. The company made no further progress towards operating to the remote destinations in its title.

Aberystwyth had already received a rail link with England in 1864. It was the current route via Machynlleth. Another line arrived later, the narrow gauge one from Devils Bridge, in 1902. Both were part of the Cambrian Railways until 1922.

The GWR took control of the C&CR in 1881 and the M&MR in 1906. The latter was purchased in 1911. The former had been extended from Llandyssul to Newcastle Emlyn on 1st June 1895.

A Light Railway Order for the Lampeter, Aberayron & New Quay Railway was obtained in October 1906 and it opened on 10th April 1911, being worked by the GWR from the outset. However, it never reached New Quay and became part of the GWR in 1922.

The GWR became the Western Region of British Railways upon nationalisation in 1948. Passenger services were withdrawn from the branches thus: Aberayron on 12th February 1951 and Newcastle Emlyn on 15th September 1952. They were lost between Aberystwyth and Strata Florida on 14th December 1964, due to flood damage. Buses were provided until the whole route closed on 22nd February 1965. The link to Llandeilo was lost in 1963. Milk traffic continued to Felin Fach and goods to Newcastle Emlyn until 1973. Details of other freight withdrawals are given in the captions.

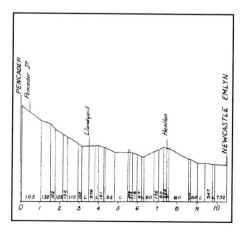

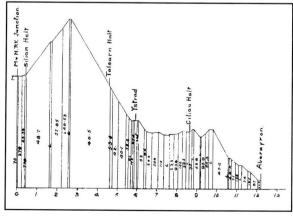

ACKNOWLEDGEMENTS

We are very grateful for the assistance received from many of those mentioned in the credits also to B.Bennett, A.R.Carder, R.Caston, G.Croughton, P.G.Gilson, S.C.Jenkins, J.John, P.Jones, P.J.Kelley, N.Langridge, B.Lewis, A.C.Mott, E.Perry, B.Robbins, Mr D. and Dr S.Salter and in particular, our ever supportive wives, Barbara Mitchell and Janet Smith.

GEOGRAPHICAL SETTING

Aberystwyth is a university town and holiday resort of great commercial importance. The line climbs from it steadily up the valley of the Afon Ystwyth for seven miles and then steeply for the next four. It crosses the watershed to enter a large area of marshland, west of the ancient abbey of Strata Florida.

An undulating course follows, close to the Afon Teifi, almost to Pencader. The river enters Cardigan Bay at Cardigan and the Newcastle Emlyn branch is mostly within the Teifi Valley. The Aberayron branch climbed out of the valley over moorland for 2½ miles, before making its long descent to the coast.

A stiff climb from Pencader for two miles takes us to another summit from which there is a long descent into the Gwili Valley and the deep ravine in which the Gwili Steam Railway has been created.

The lines north of Lampeter were built in Cardiganshire and the route south thereof in Carmarthenshire. The Newcastle Emlyn branch ran close to county borders.

The maps are to the scale of 25ins to 1 mile, with north at the top unless otherwise indicated. Welsh spelling and hyphenation has varied over the years and so we have generally used the form used by the railways at the time.

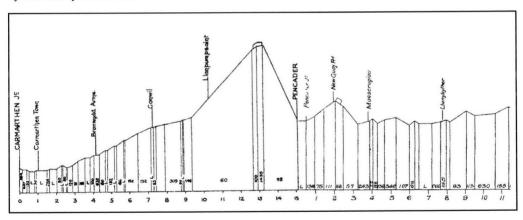

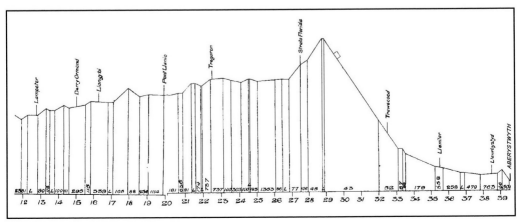

INDEX

CONTENTS

I. Map of the route showing the stations, but not the halts, in 1925.

Front cover: Brighton-built 2-6-4T no. 80100 is setting back onto its train at Pont Llanio on 26th August 1964, having removed milk tankers from it and delivered them to the nearby creamery. (D.K.Jones)

Back cover upper: The terminus at Newcastle Emlyn was recorded on 15th July 1961 and waiting to depart with goods is class 2251 0-6-0 no. 2224. The canopy had been subject to surgery for the benefit of the delivery van. (A.M.Davies)

Back cover lower: The Aberayron terminus is seen on the same day in equally pleasant surroundings. There would be goods traffic for another four years here. The engine is above the swift flowing Afon Ayron. (A.M.Davies)

Published February 2011
Reprinted October 2011

ISBN 978 1 906008 90 1

© Middleton Press, 2011

Design Deborah Esher

Published by
      Middleton Press
      Easebourne Lane
      Midhurst
      West Sussex
      GU29 9AZ
Tel: 01730 813169
Fax: 01730 812601
Email: info@middletonpress.co.uk
www.middletonpress.co.uk

Printed and bound by CPI Group (UK) Ltd, Croydon, CR0 4

ABERYSTWYTH TO CARMARTHEN

Vic Mitchell and Keith Smith

MP Middleton Press